حزب الجلجلوتية

سيدنا علي ابن ابي طالب كرم الله وجهه

THE JALJALUTIYYA LITANY

by Sayyidina Ali Ibn Abi Talib

Translated by

Dr. Ali Hussain

Foreword by

Imam Kamau Ayubbi

First Edition October 2023

ISBN: 978-1-938058-81-3

Printed in the United States of America.

Library of Congress Cataloging-in-Publication Data

TBD

Published and Distributed by:
Institute for Spiritual and Cultural Advancement
17195 Silver Parkway, #401
Fenton, MI 48430 USA
Tel: (810) 593-1222
Email: info@sufilive.com
Web: http://www.sufilive.com

Photo Credit: Joel Vodell on Unsplash

Table of Contents

بسم الله الرحمن الرحيم

بدأت ببسم الله روحي به اهتدت

الى كشف اسرار بباطنه انطوت

وصليت في الثاني على خير مرسل

محمد من زاح الضلالة والغلت

الهي لقد اقسمت باسمك داعيا

باسمائك الحسنى الاجابة حققت

الهي لقد اقسمت باسمك داعيا

روي عن بعض الائمة ان الشريف هذا ... ان الاسم ...
ولتفنا الذي هو هاهنا الاكبر ...
وهو لفظ الله شيخ

اباج يا هوج بزر كلطات سخ
باهوج هيج الاباج مرج
وبحلبوت الاجابة هلطات

سلكت بالاسم العظيم قدره
باج اهوج جلبوت هلطات باسط
بديع عظيم

الهي لقد اقسمت باسمك داعيا
باج اهوج جلباحوت تجاجات
بديع الباشر

باج

بأسمائك العظمى

باج وما هوج جل فتجلجلت

بجليل جبل جد الله جلت نسخ

الهي لقد اقسمت باسمك داعيا

باج مهوج جلجلوت تجلجلت

بحي وقيوم جليل تجلجلت صح

تقسم باسم الحي القيوم اي هو تستر بالاسم الاعظم صح

بصمصام طمطام بحرف مطلسم

بمهراش مهراش به النار اخمدت

شديد الثاني

افض لي من الانوار فيضة مشرق

على واحيي ميت قلبي بطيطفت

معناه الجبار وهو من الجبر بمعنى ع

لتحيي حيوة القلب من دنس به

العلم والمعرفة والطمانينة نسخ

وباحي باقيوم او عدت واحيا بطيطفت اموري بالهي تسلمت صح

بقيوم قام السر فيه واشرقت

على ضياء من بوارق نوره

ولاح على وجهي سناه وابرقت

اي انواره

وصب على قلبي شآبيب رحمة

بحكمة مولينا الكريم (رفعه مطر) فانطقت

احاطت بي الانوار من كل جانب

وهيبة مولانا العظيم بنا علت

فسبحانك اللهم يا خير بارئ

ويا خير خلاق ويا خير من بعث — تكرر هذا البيت

ببرهتية برهيولا بشكيلخ

بقزبمز كيدهولا اعلقمت

بال بشلع يا الهي بصعصع

كعي بمبال بنوخ تعظمت

اغثني بحفظ منك مما يضرني

وادرقني

وارزقني الميسور فيما تعسرت

بباسط وودود ان تسهل رزقنا

كريم وفتاح لرزق تسهلت

ودود وتواب برحمان بعدها

رؤف عطوف بالمحبة قد سمت

هيود قيود قد تقيد خصمنا

واقدامهم بالاسم طرا تزلزلت

بدوح بدوح حيث وذا مودة

به لي جميع العالمين تسخرت

بحق حاميم يا طلمتا اسم برهة

كرير بتليه حماه تزازغت

تم بالاسم الاعظم

واقضى الهي يا رباه بالنور حاجتي
بنور اسم جلبا سريعا
قد انقضت

باهيجا

فَبَلِّغْنِي بِقَصْدِي وَكُلَّمَا رُمْتُ

اي حاجتي

بِسِرِّ حُرُوفٍ يَا إِلٰهِي تَجَمَّعَتْ

اي اقسم عليك يا الهي بسر حروف تركيب حتى صارت كلمة وكلاما

بِسِرِّ حُرُوفٍ أُودِعَتْ فِي عَزِيمَتِي

اي همتي

عَلَوْتُ بِنُورِ الْإِسْمِ وَالرُّوحُ قَدْ عَلَتْ

أَلَا وَأَلْبِسْنِي هَيْبَةً وَجَلَالَةً

ادعوك باسمائك الحكيم

وَكُفَّ يَدَ الْأَعْدَاءِ عَنِّي بِغَلْمَهَتْ

اي الحكيم

اي كونها يا عظيما الكف يدي الاعدى شرح

أَلَا وَاحْجُبْنِي مِنْ عَدُوٍّ وَظَالِمٍ

يا رب اقضِ حاجتي

بِحَقِّ شَمَاخٍ أَشْمَخٍ سَلَتْ سَمَتْ

اي ادعوك بحرمة هذه الاسما التي علت

سلام خالق عال

وَخَلِّصْنِي مِنْ كُلِّ هَوْلٍ وَشِدَّةٍ

يا سمك النور والشديد عظيم

الا واقض يا رباه بالاسم حاجتي بنور خشم جل برهان نقضت

فَأَنْتَ غِيَاثُ الْعَالَمِينَ وَلَوْ طَغَتْ

وَسَلِّمْ بِبَحْرٍ وَأَعْطِنِي مِنْ بِرِّهَا

يا رب سلمني من هلكات بحر الدنيا

واسبل

وَاسْبِلْ عَلَى السِّتْرِ وَاشْفِ مِنَ الْغَلَثْ

غب مرضى شرح

اَصِمَّ وَاَبْكِمْ ثُمَّ اَعْمِي عَدُوَّنَا

وَاَخْرِسْهُمْ يَا ذَا الْجَلَالِ بِجَوْ سَمَتْ بمعز صادق

وَافْحِمْهُمْ مَعْ دَوْسِهِمْ وَبِرَاسِهِمْ

غنى العلى تهيب

تَحَصَّنْتُ بِالْاِسْمِ الْعَظِيمِ مِنَ الْغَلَثْ

وَاَلِّفْ قُلُوبَ الْعَالَمِينَ بِاَسْرِهِمْ

عَلَيَّ وَاَعْطِنِي الْقَبُولَ بِشَلْمَهَتْ

فتاح

وَيَسِّرْ اُمُورِي يَا اِلٰهِي وَاَعْطِنِي

مِنَ الْعِزِّ وَالْعَلْيَا بِشَنْخِ وَاشْمَخَتْ

اسم عظيم اسم اعظم

وَاسْبِلْ عَلَيْنَا السِّتْرَ وَاشْفِ قُلُوبَنَا

وَاَنْتَ شِفَاءُ الْقُلُوبِ مِنَ الْغَلَثِ الْخَبَثْ

اى مرض

اى عدوى ممنعا شر المسلمين والمرء وعجزه وازالة مملكته فى الارض اى الاضرار والاذلال والافنان اى واجعله عاجزا حتى لا يقدر علينا كمن هو اخذ كره وليسانه وعينه شرح

اى اسئلك يا ذا الجلال باسمك الصادق لانك المجيب الصادق الكريم شرح

وهو الذي يفتح بعنايته كل مخلوق من عالم الملك والملكوت والامور والهيرة بعض الانبياء عليهم السلام ويفتح قلوب اوليائه اما الملكوت بالمكاشفة شرح

وبارك لنا اللهم في جميع كسبنا
وحل عقود العسر يا بوه ارتجت (اعلقت)
بيا بوه ويا بوه ويا خير بازخ
وبامن لنا الارزاق من جوده نمت (زادت)
نرد بك الاعداء من كل وجهة
وبالبؤس ترميهم من البعد بالشتت
واخز لهموا يا ذا الجلال بفضل من
اليه سعت ضب الفلاة قد اشتكت

توسل سيد الانام عزم

فانك رجائي يا الهي وسيدي
ففرق لميم الجيش ان رام بي عنت
وكف جميع المضرين (اي ضرر) من كيدهم

عني

عني باقسامك حتما وما حوت

فيا خير مسؤل واكرم من عطى

ويا خير مامول الى امة خلت

بتعداد ايد شم سنداب بيطح

اماا وبهرات بلام تبركت اى تبرزت

اقذ كوكبي بالاسم نورا وبهجة

مدا الدهر والايام يانور جلجلت

يانور

بآج اهوج جلمهوج جلالة

ابد عظيم هو قدرا

جليل جل جليوت جما تمهرجت

تقاد سراج النرج سرا بيانة

ظاهر

تقاد سرج النرج سرا تنورت

بالنور

قسم باسمه تعالى

بتعداد ابروم وبيمراز ابرم

معيد

وبهرة تبرين وافرتبركت

نكرر الاسم الشريف المعيد

بنور بمال بازخ وشرنطخ

نور ساطع

بقدوس برهوت به الظلمة انجلت

بال اهيل شلع شلعوب شالع

برحمن رحيم حق

طهي طهوب طيطهوب تطيطمت

الى بنور جمال الرافة

جميل

مجيب

انوخ بيملوخ وابروخ اقسمت

ورد الثاني الاهو الانفاع التجمل الى الحبيب

بتمليخ ابات شموخ نشلمت

العالي

اباريخ بيذوخ وديموخ بعدها

خماروخ بشروخ بشرخ تنغمت

اقسام بالاسما النورانيه

ببلخ وسمیان وبازوخ بعدها

بز بوخ

بزيموخ اشموخ به الكون عمرت

وكيل فرد

بشلمخت اقبل دعائي وكن معي

يارب

وكن لي من الاعداء حسبي فقد بغت

انوخ بيملوخ بروخ وبرخوا

قدير قادر معيد

بتملاخ ياياه شموخ تشامخت

علام عال تعالت

فيا شملخا يا شملخا انت شملخا

الرحمن

ويا عيطلا غوث الرياح تخلخلت

علاء علت الامزاج القوي

ويا تملخا ياه فها انت تملخا

ويا شمخشتا تلك ذات تنورت

عظيم النور

بياه ويايوه نوره اصاليا

صمد

بجا غاليا يسر اموري بصلصلت

سريع ذوالبطش

وَلْحُرُسْنِي يَاذَا الْجَلَالِ بِكُنْ وَكُنْ

اي احفظني من كل جبار عنيد وشيطان مريد قوله كن فكون

بِنَقْشٍ حَكِيمٍ قَاطِعِ الشَّرِّ اُسْبِتَتْ

واحرسني يا ذا الجلال كرامة بامرار علم زين قلبي وقربت

بِكَ الْحَوْلُ وَالطَّوْلُ الشَّدِيدُ لِمَنْ اَتَى

لِبَابِكَ يَرْجُو جَاهَكَ الظُّلْمَةُ انْجَلَتْ

حُرُوفٌ لِبَهْرَامٍ عَلَتْ وَتَشَامَخَتْ

بِاَسْمَاءِ عَصُومُوشِي الظُّلْمَةُ انْجَلَتْ

التوسل بالاقسام المستجابة الجليلة

تَوَسَّلْتُ بِالْاَقْسَامِ رَبِّي بِحَقِّهَا

بِفَضْلِ جَلَالِ اللّٰهِ بِالْخَيْرِ قَدْ اَتَتْ

بِحَقِّ لَمَطْهَطِيلٍ مَهْطَهْطِيلٍ بَعْدَهَا

اسما التهاطيل صح

بِحَقِّ قَهْطَهْطِيلٍ فَهْطَهْطِيلٍ اَرْبَعَتْ

بِحَقِّ نَهْطَهْطِيلٍ جَهْطَهْطِيلٍ سَادِسٍ

بحق

بحق لهطهطيل لقفنجل جمعت

ملكت بميم الملك سيفا مجردا

اصول به قهرا على الانس والجن اذ بغت

وقومني القيوم بالقاف قاهرا

ظهورا للاعداء والرقاب تقطعت

المروة لله لا شيء غيره

حببت لنور الروح والاسم قد علت

اي جلت

فتلك حروف النور فاجمع خواصها

وحقق معانيها بها الخير تمت

اوائل سور الذكر تقرا فواتحا

لاشراق مافيها من النور اشرقت

اي حروف هو هذه الاحرف حروف النورانية

وفيها سر لا يعلمه

بألفٍ ولامٍ ثمّ ميمٍ على الولا

أنالُ بها ما تشتهي النفسُ وسعتْ

بألفٍ ولامٍ والنساءِ عقودُها

وفي سورةِ الأنعامِ والنورِ نوّرتْ

بألفٍ ولامٍ ثمّ ميمٍ وصادِها

علوتُ بها فخراً وذاك تنوّرتْ

بألفٍ ولامٍ ثمّ راءٍ بسترِها

علوتُ بنورِ الاسمِ من كلِّ ما خبتْ

بألفٍ ولامٍ ثمّ ميمٍ ورائِها

إلى مجمعِ الأرواحِ والروحُ قد علتْ

بكافٍ وهايا ثمّ عينٍ وصادِها

كفا يتنا

كفايتنا من كل عين بنا حوت
بطه ويا سين وطسين تكن لنا
وطاسين ميم بالسعادة اقبلت
بسر حواميم الكتاب جميعها
عليك بفضل النور يا نور اقسمت
بحاميم عين ثم بسين وقافها
حمايتنا من كل سوء تسلمت
بقاف ونون ثم حاميم بعدها
وفي سورة الدخان سرا قد حكمت
والذاريات ذروا والنجم اذا هوى
وباقتربت لي الامور تقربت

بِحَقِّ تَبَارَكَ ثُمَّ نُونٍ وَسَآئِلٍ

وَفِي سُورَةِ التَّطْفِيفِ وَالشَّمْسُ كُوِّرَتْ

بِعَمَّ وَعَبَسَ وَالنَّازِعَاتِ وَطَارِقٍ

وَفِي السَّمَآءِ ذَاتِ الْبُرُوجِ وَزُلْزِلَتْ

وَفِي سُورَةِ الْقُرْآنِ حَرْفًا مُجَرَّدًا أَيِ الْفُرْقَانِ

أَيْ وَآيَةً

عَدَدَ مَا قَرَى الْقَارِي وَمَا قَدْ تَنَزَّلَتْ

سَأَلْتُكَ يَا مَوْلَايَ فِي فَضْلِكَ الَّذِي

عَلَى كُلِّ مَآ أَنْزَلْتَ كِتَابًا تَفَضَّلَتْ

بِأَهْيَا شَرَاهِيَا أَدُونَايِ صَبَوَةٍ

بِعِزَّةِ آلِ شَدَّاي قَدْ تَجَمَّعَتْ

بِسِرِّ بَدُوحٍ أَجْهَزَطٍ بَطَدٍ زَهَجٍ

بواح

بولج الوحا والنصر والفتح قد حوت

بفرد وجبار شهيد وناربت

ظهير خبير بزكي تجمعت

بحق فتح مع فخمت يا الهنا

باسمائك العظمى اجرنا من الشتت

بنور فجش مع تظنخز يا سيدى

وبالاية الكرسى آمنى من الفجت

بنور جلال ونور جمال الهى وسيدى

وبالاية الكبرى امنى من الفجت

توسلت اليك مولانا بسرها

توسل ذى ذل به الناس اهتدت

حروف بمعناها لها الفضل شرفت

مدد الدهر والايام يارب انجلت

فسخر لي فيها خديما يطيعني

بفضل حروف ام القران وما تلت — اى الكتاب

بفضل كتاب الله بالقدرة التى

بها الارض مدت والجبال تشمخت

بحقك بالاملاك والرسل كلهم

بحرمة يوم الحشر والخلق جمعت

بياء ونون مع واو جميعها

بكشف هلكتاخ كنون تكونت

واسئلك يامولاى في اسمك الذى

بِهِ إِذْ دُعَاىِ جَمْعُ الْأُمُورِ تَيَسَّرَتْ

وَتَرْحَمُ ضَعْفِي يَا إِلٰهِي وَذِلَّتِي

بِمَا قَدْ دَعَاكَ الْأَنْبِيَاءُ تَوَسَّلَتْ

أَيَا خَالِقِي وَيَا سَيِّدِي اقْضِ حَاجَتِي

إِلَيْكَ أُمُورِي يَا إِلٰهِي تَسَلَّمَتْ

تَوَسَّلْتُ يَا رَبِّي إِلَيْكَ بِأَحْمَدِ

وَأَسْمَائِكَ الْحُسْنَى الَّتِي هِيَ جُمِعَتْ

لَا إِلٰهَ إِلَّا اللهُ أَنْتَ يَا حَيُّ يَا قَيُّومُ

وَأَنْتَ حَسْبِي رَبِّ جَلَّ اللهُ جَلْجَلَتْ

فَجُدْ وَاعْفُ وَامْنَحْ يَا إِلٰهِي بِتَوْبَةٍ

عَلَى عَبْدِكَ الْمِسْكِينِ مِنْ نَظْرَةٍ تَمَّتْ

زادت

وللخير وفقني وللصدق والتقى

واسكني الفردوس مع فرقة علت

وكن لي رؤوفا في حياتي وبعدما

اموت وارفع ظلمة القبر والخلت

وفي الحشر يا الهي بيض صحيفتي

وثقل موازيني بفضلك وانجلت

وجوزني على حد الصراط مصرولا

فيحفظني من حر نار وما حوت

تسامحني من كل ذنب جنيته

وتعف عن خطيئاتي العظام وان علت

ثلاث عصي صففت بعد خاتم

على

عَلَى رَأْسِهَا مِثْلُ السِّنَانِ تَنَزَّكَتْ

وَمِيمٌ طَمِيسٌ أَبْتَرٌ ثُمَّ سُلَّمٌ

وَفِي وَسْطِهَا بِالْحَرْبَتَيْنِ تَقَوَّمَتْ

وَأَرْبَعَةٌ تَحْكِي الْأَنَامِلَ بَعْدَهَا

تُشِيرُ إِلَى الْخَيْرَاتِ وَالرِّزْقِ جُمِّعَتْ

وَهَاءٌ شَقِيقٌ ثُمَّ وَاوٌ مُقَوَّسٌ

كَأُنْبُوبِ حَجَّامٍ مِنَ السِّرِّ النُّوتْ

وَآخِرُهَا مِثْلُ الْأَوَائِلِ خَاتَمٌ

خُمَاسِيُّ أَرْكَانٍ بِهِ السِّرُّ قَدْ حَوَتْ

وَلَا إِلَهَ إِلَّا اللهُ جَلَّ جَلَالُهُ

مُحَمَّدٌ رَسُولُ اللهِ حَقًّا وَحُقِّقَتْ

تم

تمت بقلم الفقير اليه تعالى جل جلاله محمد متولي

عفي عنه

المصري الكاتب بالجامع الازهر الانور سنة ١٢٧١

بِسْمِ ٱللَّهِ ٱلرَّحْمَٰنِ ٱلرَّحِيمِ

Foreword

"If you read the Jaljalutiyya, then you have read all of creation!"
Shaykh Muhammad Hisham Kabbani

Reading is not simply an act of uttering letters and yet, it is. When we pronounce, there is an announcement flowing through the fields of our being, forms and blood, into our nervous system and even the patterns of our lives moving through time and space back to our years of development, heedlessness, efforts, childhood triumphs and traumas, even our fetal development in the subconscious recesses of our soul.

That pronouncement may reverberate back to the coded genome of our ancestors. And yet, all these patterns and stories can take us even further into the fields and patterns before the creation of our forms.

The sounds of *jīm*, *lām*, or *jalla* reverberate and bounce through our teeth and tongue as energy that is held by God Almighty, between majesty and beauty, *jalāl* and *jamāl*.

When the *mīm* flickers in appearance of the seen and unseen, it trades places between the heavenly majesty of Ahmad ﷺ and mercy of Muhammad ﷺ, causing the heart to stir in rotation, as it searches for its destination. Furthermore, these sounds and meanings take us on a journey and quest for the roots of creation and its appearances.

It is here that *al-Asmā' al-Ḥusnā* (the Most Beautiful Divine Names) call for our attention and remembrance to bring us back in the direction of our origin.

Therefore, sacred sound must not be read analytically for the sake of control or comprehension, but with the intention of entering a space of intimate sparks of Divine Reality.

This prayer, the *Jaljalūtiyya*, carries sounds and letters anchored in the Beautiful and Majestic Names of our Origin, sustenance, protection, guidance, and evolving journey.

Its rhyming phrases resonate from a heart that is not attached to this world of forms and density, but one that absorbs the dense meanings of subtle worlds translated in supplying and supplicating words.

These phrases, attributed to the spiritual knight and inheritor of Muhammadan Light, our master Ali Ibn Abi Talib ﷻ, carry a weight and resonance that demand a heart moved by the Love and Beauty of Allah, so as not to clash with His Majesty, but rather come under His Care and Protection.

These are words that come at an opportune time, when we are in dire need of a shelter to cultivate, protect and nurture the Light of the soul. It is in this spirit that I believe this text has been translated and transliterated for our benefit.

Chaplain Kamau Ayubbi
Detroit, Michigan
October 25, 2023 (10th of Rabiʿ al-Thani, 1445)

بِسْمِ ٱللَّهِ ٱلرَّحْمَٰنِ ٱلرَّحِيمِ

Introduction

All praise is due to Allah who facilitates for His servants to love Him, only because He loved them first. The height of that love manifests in prophets and messengers, most auspiciously in their master and leader, our beloved Muhammad ﷺ, his family, companions and those who follow them in guidance until the end of time.

The most auspicious among these is *bāb madīnatu-l-ʿilm* (the gate to the city of knowledge), son-in-law and cousin of the Prophet ﷺ, Sayyidina Ali ibn Abi Talib عليه السلام, may God be pleased with him and his progeny eternally. Not enough words can be spent praising and enumerating the praiseworthy traits of the husband of our lady Fatima al-Zahra عليها السلام, the daughter of the Prophet ﷺ about whom he ﷺ said: "Fatima is a part of me" and "she is the mother of her father."

All springs of Islamic *ʿaqīda* (theology), *fiqh* (jurisprudence) and *taṣawwuf* (spirituality) find their origin in the heart of this 'gate to the city of knowledge', our master Ali Ibn Abi Talib عليه السلام, which he took directly from the heart of the Prophet ﷺ. In the case of *fiqh* (jurisprudence), we find Imam al-Shafiʿi رضي الله عنه learning from the granddaughter of the Prophet ﷺ

and daughter of Sayyidina Ali ﷺ, our lady Sayyida Nafisa ﷺ in Egypt.

In *ʿaqīda* (theology), the prominent Muslim theologian Imam Abu al-Hasan al-Basri ﷺ was a student of our master Ali ﷺ, whereas in *taṣawwuf* (spirituality), all Sufi *ṭuruq* (paths) trace their *silsila* (lineage) to Sayyidina Ali ﷺ, save for the Naqshbandiyya path that traces its origin to our master Abu Bakr al-Siddiq ﷺ. However, even in this Sufi path, the fifth saint in its 'golden chain' is none other than our master Jaʿfar al-Sadiq ﷺ, the son of our master Muhammad al-Baqir ﷺ, the son of our master Ali Zaynul ʿAbideen ﷺ, son of our master Hussain ﷺ, the jewel of his grandfather the Prophet ﷺ and son of our master Ali ﷺ.

Among the countless knowledges that the Prophet ﷺ deposited in the heart of Sayyidina Ali ﷺ are the spiritual secrets that connect heaven and earth, the breaths that undergird the sounds and voices of the Qurʾan, God's final testament and revelation to humanity. All of these can be found in the litany at hand: *al-Jaljalūtiyya*. This prayer should be considered the source and origin of the countless supplications written by Muslim saints throughout history, many of whom were themselves descendants of Sayyidina Ali ﷺ.

The poignant spiritual potency of this prayer is due to the inundated use of *suryāniyya*, a language that Muslim saints describe as the tongue of the higher realm, of angels and other spiritual beings. Particularly, *al-Jaljalūtiyya* is filled with *Barhatiyyāt*, or names of God in *suryāniyya*, as well as the names of other high-ranking angels.

The primary purpose of this prayer is definitive protection, as is mentioned in the following verses from the litany that, despite not being found in the original manuscript, were nonetheless added in this edition in bold:

You, who carries the Lofty Name
Fulfill your needs, through it all affairs are safe
Do not fear a sword nor the stab of a knife
And fear neither a spear nor evil's arrow
And fear neither a snake nor a scorpion you see
Nor a roaring lion that leaps at you
Fight, do not be frightened and battle without fear
And step upon every land filled with monsters
Come forth, do not run away
and show enmity to whomever you will
Do not fear the might of kings even if they overwhelm you

Many of these names and terms in *suryāniyya* have been rendered in, as far as I know, the only English translation and transliteration of *al-Jaljalūtiyya*. This litany's protective potency is so widespread and known among Muslim saints that Mawlana Shaykh Nazim, may God sanctify his secret, advised one of his grandsons to recite it daily.

I offer it here with the hope that as many Muslims around the world recite it with the intention of lifting the oppression and injustice that has befallen humanity. That we recognize our need to seek the rectification of our affairs in the physical world by turning to the source: God's help and the spiritual realm.

وآخِرُ دَعْوَانَا أَنْ الحَمْدُ لله رَبِّ العَالَمِينْ

وَ مَا تَوْفِيقِي إِلَّا بالله

بِسْمِ ٱللَّهِ ٱلرَّحْمَٰنِ ٱلرَّحِيمِ

Bismillāh ar-Raḥmān ar-Raḥīm
In the Name of Allah,
Most-Beneficent, Most Merciful

الحَمْدُ لله رَبِّ العَالَمِينَ

وَالصَّلاةُ وَالسَّلامُ عَلَى سَيِّدِنَا مُحَمَّدٍ وَعَلى آلِهِ وَصَحْبِهِ أَجْمَعِينْ

Al-ḥamdu lillāhi Rabbil ʿālamīn wa-ṣ-ṣalātu wa-s-salāmu ʿalā sayyidinā Muḥammadin wa ʿalā ālihi wa ṣahbihi ajmaʿīn
All Praise is due to Allah, the Lord of the Worlds. Immense Prayers and Salutations upon our Master Muhammad ﷺ, his family and companions in their entirety.

حزب الجلجلوتية

Ḥizb al-Jaljalūtiyyah
The Jaljalutiyya Litany

بَدَأْتُ بِبِسْمِ اللهِ رُوحِي بِهِ اهْتَدَتْ

Badaʾtu bi-bismillāhi rūḥī bihi-htadat
I begin by God's Name through whom my spirit is guided

إِلَى كَشْفِ أَسْرَارٍ بِبَاطِنِهِ انْطَوَتْ

Ilā kashfi asrārin bi-bāṭinihi-nṭawat
To unveil secrets, in whose Essence they have subsided

وَصَلَّيْتُ فِي الثَّانِي عَلَى خَيْرِ مُرْسَلٍ

Wa ṣallaytu fi-ththānī ʿalā khayri mursalin
I send benedictions upon the best of messengers

مُحَمَّدٌ مَنْ زَاحَ الضَّلَالَةَ وَالْغَلَتْ

Muḥammadun man zāḥ-a-ḍḍalālata wa-l-ghalat
Muhammad ﷺ who removed darkness and faults

إِلَهِي لَقَدْ أَقْسَمْتُ بِاسْمِكَ دَاعِيًا

Ilāhī laqad aqsamtu bi-smika dāʿiyan
O God, I attest by your Name and supplicate

بِأَسْمَائِكَ الْحُسْنَى الْإِجَابَةِ حُقِّقَتْ

Bi-asmāʾika-l-ḥusna-l-ijābati ḥuqqiqat
Through Your Names of Beauty response is assured

إِلَهِي لَقَدْ أَقْسَمْتُ بِاسْمِكَ دَاعِيًا

Ilāhī laqad aqsamtu bi-smika dāʿiyan
O God, I attest by your Name and supplicate

بِآجٍ وَمَاهُوجٍ جَلَّ فَتَجَلْجَلَتْ

Bi-ājin wa māhūjin jalla fa-tajaljalat
By the Most-Exalted, Beautiful and Elevated

إِلَهِي لَقَدْ أَقْسَمْتُ بِاسْمِكَ دَاعِيًا

Ilāhī laqad aqsamtu bi-smika dāʿiyan
O God, I attest by your Name and supplicate

بِآجٍ مَهُوجٍ جَلْجَلُوتٍ تَجَلْجَلَتْ

Bi-ājin mahūjin jaljalūtin tajaljalat
By the All-Living, Everlasting and Most-Exalted

بِصَمْصَامٍ طَمْطَامٍ بِحَرْفٍ مُطَلْسَمٍ

Bi-ṣamṣāmin ṭamṭāmin bi-ḥarfin muṭalsamin

By Samsam and Tamtam and an encrypted letter

بِمَهْرَاشٍ مَهْرَاشٍ بِهِ النَّارُ أُخْمِدَتْ

Bi-mahrāshin mahrāshin bihi-n-nāru ukhmidat

By the Most-Strong through whom fire is extinguished

أَفِضْ لِيَ مِنَ الْأَنْوَارِ فَيْضَةَ مُشْرِقٍ

Afiḍ liya min-al-anwāri fayḍata mushriqin

Overflow upon me from lights a flood of illumination

عَلَيَّ وَأَحْيِي مَيْتَ قَلْبِي بِطَيْطَفَتْ

ʿAlayya wa aḥyī mayta qalbī bi-ṭayṭafat

Upon me and enliven my heart's death, O All-Powerful

لِتُحْيِيَ حَيَاةَ الْقَلْبِ مِنْ دَنَسٍ بِهِ

Li-tuḥyiya ḥayāta-l-qalbi min danasin bihi

To enliven a heart's life away from its filth

بِقَيُّومٍ قَامَ السِّرُّ فِيهِ وَأَشْرَقَتْ

Bi-Qayyūmin qāma-s-sirru fīhi wa ashraqat

Through the Everlasting through whom
the secret persevered and glowed

عَلَيَّ ضِيَاءٌ مِنْ بَوَارِقِ نُورِهِ

ʿAlayya ḍiyāʾun min bawāriqi nūrihi

Upon me there is a light from His Light, it glimpsed

وَلَاحَ عَلَى وَجْهِي سَنَاهُ وَأَبْرَقَتْ

Wa lāḥa ʿalā wajhī sanāhu wa abraqat
And upon my face appeared His Countenance, it lightened

وَصُبَّ عَلَى قَلْبِي شَبَابِيبَ رَحْمَةٍ

Wa ṣubba ʿalā qalbī shababībа raḥmatin
Cast upon my heart youthful mercy

بِحِكْمَةِ مَوْلَانَا الْكَرِيمُ فَانْطَقَتْ

Bi-ḥikmati Mawlāna-l-Karīmu fa-nṭaqat
An utterance of wisdom from Our Generous Guardian

أَحَاطَتْ بِيَ الْأَنْوَارُ مِنْ كُلِّ جَانِبٍ

Aḥāṭat biya-l-anwāru min kulli jānibin
The lights surrounded me from every side

وَهَيْبَةُ مَوْلَانَا الْعَظِيمُ بِنَا عَلَتْ

Wa haybatu Mawlāna-l-ʿAẓīmu binā ʿalat
And the aura of the Great Guardian elevated us

فَسُبْحَانَكَ اللّٰهُمَّ يَا خَيْرَ بَارِئٍ

Fa-subḥānaka Allāhumma yā khayra Bāriʾin
So, Glory be to You, O God, the Best Creator

وَيَا خَيْرَ خَلَّاقٍ وَيَا خَيْرَ مَنْ بَعَثْ

Wa yā khayra Khallāqin wa yā khayra man baʿat
O Best of Innovators and Best of Givers

بِبَرْهَتِيَّةٍ بَرْهَيُولًا بِشَكَيْلَخٍ

Bi-Barhatiyyatin Barhayūlan bi-Shakaylakhin
Through a Barhatiyya, Barhayula and Shakaylakh

بِقَزٍّ بِمَزٍّ كَيْدَهُولًا اَعَلْقَمَتْ

Bi-Qazzin bi-Mazzin Kaydahūlan aʿalqamat
Through a Qazz, Mazz, Kaydahul and Aʿalqamat

بِآلٍ بِشَلْعٍ يَا إِلَهِي بِصَعْصَعٍ

Bi-Ālin bi-Shalʿin yā Ilāhī bi-Ṣaʿṣaʿin
Through an Al, Shalʿ, my Lord and Ṣaʿṣaʿ

كَعَيٍّ بِمِمْيَالٍ بَنُوخٍ تَعَظَّمَتْ

Ka-ʿAyyin bi-Mimyālin Banūkhin Taʿaẓẓamat
Like an ʿAyy through a Mimyāl, a Banūkh Exalted

اَغِثْنِي بِحِفْظٍ مِنْكَ مِمَّا يَضُرُّنِي

Aghithnī bi-ḥifẓin minka mimmā yaḍurrunī
Save me, through Your Protection, from what harms me

وَارْزُقْنِيَ المَيْسُورَ فِيمَا تَعَسَّرَتْ

Wa-rzuqnī-l-maysūra fī-mā taʿassarat
Sustain me with ease in my difficulties

بِبَاسِطٍ وَدُودٍ اِنْ تُسَهِّلَ رِزْقَنَا

Bi-Bāsiṭin Wadūdin in tusahhila rizqanā
O Expander and Most-Loving,
if you facilitate our sustenance

كَرِيمٌ وَفَتَّاحٌ لِرِزْقِي تَسَهَّلَتْ

Karīmun wa Fattāḥun li-rizqī tasahhalat
Most-Generous and Opener, my sustenance is facilitated

وَدُودٌ وَتَوَّابٌ بِرَحْمَانَ بَعْدَهَا

Wadūdun wa Tawwābun bi-Raḥmāna baʿdahā
Most-Loving, Forgiving and thenceforth Merciful

رَؤُوفٌ عَطُوفٌ بِالمَحَبَّةِ قَدْ سَمَتْ

Raʾūfun ʿAṭūfun bi-l-Maḥabbati qad samat
Most-Kind and Caring, with love in ascent

هَيُودٌ قَيُودٍ قَدْ تَقَيَّدَ خَصْمُنَا

Hayūdun Qayūdin qad taqayyada khaṣmunā
Hayud, Qayud, our enemies have been chained

وَأَقْدَامُهُمْ بِالِاسْمِ طُرًّا تَزَلْزَلَتْ

Wa aqdāmahum bi-l-Ismi ṭurran tazalzalat
Their feet, through the Name, suddenly shook

بَدُّوحٌ بَدُّوحٌ حَيْثُ وُدًّا مَوَدَّةً

Baddūḥun Baddūḥun ḥaythu wudhdhan mawaddatan
Baduh, Baduh wherein is kindness and love

بِهِ لِي جَمِيعُ الْعَالَمِينَ تَسَخَّرَتْ

Bihi lī jamīʿul ʿālamīna tasakhkharat
Through which all the world aided me

بِحَقِّ حَامِيمٍ يَا طَلْخَتَا اِسْمُ بَرْهَةٍ

Bi-Ḥaqqi Ḥāmīmin yā Ṭalkhatā ismu barhatin
By the right of Ha-Mim, O Talkhata, the name of Barhat

كَرِيرٍ بِتَتْلِيْهٍ حِمَاهُ تَزَازَغَتْ

Karīrin bi-Tatlīhin Ḥimāhun tazāzaghat
Karir, with a Tatlih, fortresses dispersed

فَبَلِّغْنِي بِقَصْدِي وَكُلَّ مَأْرِبِي

Fa-ballighnī bi-qaṣdī wa kulla maʾribī
Grant me through my intention and all my desires

بِسِرِّ حُرُوفٍ يَا إِلَهِي تَجَمَّعَتْ

Bi-sirri ḥurūfin yā ilāhī tajammaʿat
Through the secret of letters, my Lord, that gathered

بِسِرِّ حُرُوفٍ أُودِعَتْ فِي عَزِيمَتِي

Bi-sirri ḥurūfin ūdiʿat fī ʿazīmatī
Through the secret of letters placed in my resolve

عَلَوْتُ بِنُورِ الْإِسْمِ وَالرُّوحِ قَدْ عَلَتْ

ʿAlawtu bi-nūri-l-Ismi wa-r-rūḥu qad ʿalat
I elevated through the Name's Light as did my spirit

أَلَا وَأَلْبِسَانِي هَيْبَةً وَجَلَالَةً

Alā wa albisānī haybatan wa jalālatan
Dress me in awe and majesty

وَكُفَّ يَدَيِ الْأَعْدَاءِ عَنِّي بِغَلْمَهَتْ

Wa kuffa yadayi-l-aʿdāʾi ʿannī bi-Ghalmahat
Deter the enemies' hands away from me, O Most-Wise

أَلَا وَاحْجُبَانِي مِنْ عَدُوٍّ وَظَالِمٍ

Alā wa-ḥjubānī min ʿaduwwin wa ẓālimin
Veil me from every enemy and transgressor

بِحَقِّ شَمَاخٍ أَشْمَخٍ سَلْمَتْ سَمَتْ

Bi-ḥaqqi Shamākhin Ashmakhin salmat samat
By the status of the Lofty, Creator, Peace in ascent

وَخَلِّصْنِي مِنْ كُلِّ هَوْلٍ وَشِدَّةٍ

Wa khalliṣnī min kulli hawlin wa shiddatin
Save me from every calamity and difficulty

فَأَنْتَ غِيَاثُ الْعَالَمِينَ وَلَوْ طَغَتْ

Fa-anta ghiyāthu-l-ʿālamīna wa law ṭaghat
You are the salvation of the world if they transgress

وَسَلِّمْ بِبَحْرٍ وَاَعْطِنِي خَيْرَ بَرِّهَا

Wa sallim bi-baḥrin wa aʿṭinī khayra barrihā
Grant safety with the sea and grant me the best of its land

وَاسْبُلْ عَلَيَّ السِّرَ وَاشْفِ مِنَ الْغَلَتْ

Wa-sbul ʿalayya-s-sirra wa-shfi mina-l-ghalat
Cast upon me the secret and cure me of fault

أَصِمَّ وَأَبْكِمْ ثُمَّ أَعْمِ عَدُوَّنَا

Aṣimma wa abkim thumma aʿmi ʿaduwwanā
Mute, Deafen and blind our enemy

وَاخْرِسْهُمْ يَا ذَا الْجَلَالِ بِحَوْسَمَتْ

Wa-khrishum yā Dha-l-Jalāli bi-Ḥawsamat
Silence them, O Most-Majestic, through Truth

وَفِي حَوْسَمٍ مَعَ دَوْسَمٍ وَبَرَاسَمٍ

Wa fī Ḥawsamin maʿa Dawsamin wa Barāsamin
Through the Apparent, Lofty and Most-Wise

تَحَصَّنْتُ بِالْاِسْمِ الْعَظِيمِ مِنَ الْغَلَتْ

Taḥaṣṣantu bi-l-Ismi-l-Aẓīmi mina-l-ghalat
I seek protection through the Great Name from faults

وَأَلِّفْ قُلُوبَ الْعَالَمِينَ بِأَسْرِهِمْ

Wa allif qulūba-l-ʿālamīna bi asrihim
Unite the hearts of people in their entirety

عَلَيَّ وَاَعْطِنِي الْقَبُولَ بِشَلْمَهَتْ

ʿAlayya wa aʿṭini-l-qabūla bi-Shalmahat
Upon me and grant me acceptance, O Opener

وَيَسِّرْ أُمُورِي يَا إِلَهِي وَاَعْطِنِي

Wa yassir umūrī yā Ilāhī wa-aʿṭinī
Facilitate my affairs, O my Lord, and grant me

مِنَ الْعِزِّ وَالْعُلْيَا بِشَمْخٍ وَاشْمَخَتْ

Mina-l- ʿizzi wa-l- ʿulyā bi-Shamkhin wa Ashmakhat
Of exaltedness and loftiness through the Great and Greater

وَاسْبِلْ عَلَيْنَا السِّرَّ وَاشْفِ قُلُوبَنَا

Wa-sbil ʿalayna-s-sirra wa-shfi qulūbanā
Cast upon us the secret and cure our hearts

وَأَنْتَ شِفَاءُ الْقُلُوبِ مِنَ الْغَلَتْ

Wa anta shifāʾu-l-qulūbi mina-l-ghalat
Indeed, You are the hearts' cure from faults

وَبَارِكْ لَنَا اللّٰهُمَّ فِي جَمِيعِ كَسْبِنَا

Wa bārik Allāhumma lanā fī jamīʿi kasbinā
Bless us, O God, in all our wealth

وَحُلَّ عُقُودَ الْعُسْرِ يَايُوهٍ اِرْتَجَتْ

Wa ḥulla ʿuqūda-l- ʿusri yā-Yūhin irtajat
And untie the knots of difficulty,
O our Aid, we ask You

بِيَايُوهٍ وَيَايُوهٍ وَيَا خَيْرَ بَازِخٍ

Bi-Yāyūhin wa Yāyūhin wa yā khayra bāzikhin
O our Aid, O our Aid, and the Best of Knowers

وَيَا مَنْ لَنَا الْأَرْزَاقُ مِنْ جُودِهِ نَمَتْ

Wa yā man lana-l-arzāqu min jūdihi namat
O You through whose munificence, our wealth grows

نَرُدُّ بِكَ الْأَعْدَاءَ مِنْ كُلِّ وُجْهَةٍ

Naruddu bika-l-aʿdāʾu min kulli wujhatin

We deter enemies from every path through You

وَبِالْبُؤْسِ تَرْمِيهِمْ مِنَ الْبُعْدِ بِالشَّتَتْ

Wa bi-l-buʾsi tarmīhim mina-l-buʿdi bi-sh-shatat

With severity You cast them in distance and dispersion

وَاخْذِلْهُمُوا يَا ذَا الْجَلَالِ بِفَضْلِ مَنْ

Wa-khdhilhumū yā Dha-l-Jalāli bi-faḍli man

And humiliate them, O Majestic One, by the nobility of

إِلَيْهِ سَعَتْ ضَبُّ الْفَلَاةِ قَدِ اشْتَكَتْ

Ilayhi saʿat ḍabbu-l-falāti qad-i-shtakat

He to whom the lizard in the desert complained

فَأَنَّكَ رَجَائِي يَا إِلَٰهِي وَسَيِّدِي

Fa-annaka rajāʾī yā Ilāhī wa Sayyidī

Indeed, You are my Hope, O my Lord and Master

فَفَرِّقْ لَمِيمَ الْجَيْشِ إِنْ رَامَ بِي عَنَتْ

Fa-farriq lamīma-l-jayshi in rāma bī ʿanat

Disperse the gathering of armies when they overwhelm me

وَكُفَّ جَمِيعَ الْمُضَرِّينَ مِنْ كَيْدِهِمْ

Wa kuffa jamīʿa-l-muḍarrīna min kaydihim

Turn away all those who intend harm

عَنِّي بِأَقْسَامِكَ حَتْمًا وَمَا حَوَتْ

ʿAnnī bi-aqsāmika ḥatman wa mā ḥawat
From me, through your oaths
and what they contain, with certainty

فَيَا خَيْرَ مَسْؤُولٍ وَأَكْرَمُ مَنْ عَطَى

Fa-yā khayra masʾūlin wa akramu man ʿaṭā
O Best of those Sought and Most Generous of Givers

وَيَا خَيْرَ مَأْمُولٍ إِلَى أُمَّةٍ خَلَتْ

Wa yā khayra maʾmūlin ilā ummatin khalat
And the Best of Hopes for a last nation

بِتَعْدَادِ أَيْدٍ ثُمَّ سِنْدَابِ بَيْطَمٍ

Bi-taʿdādi aydin thumma Sindābi Bayṭamin
By the numbers of Divine Hands and a Strong Baytam

آمَاءٍ وَبَهْرَاتٍ بِلَامٍ تَبَرَّكَتْ

Āmāʾin wa Bahrātin bi-lāmin tabarrakat
Amaʾin and Bahratin and with a manifest Lam

أَقِدْ كَوْكَبِي بِالْاِسْمِ نُورًا وَبَهْجَةً

Aqid kawkabī bi-l-Ismi nūran wa bahjatan
Ignite my star, through the Name, in light and joy

مَدَا الدَّهْرِ وَالْأَيَّامِ يَا نُورُ جَلْجَلَتْ

Mada-d-dahri wa-l-ayyāmi yā Nurū Jaljalat
Throughout time and days, O Light of Lights

بِآجٍ أَهُوجٍ جَلْمَهُوجٍ جَلَالَةً

Bi-Ājin Ahūjin Jalmahūjin jalālatan
O God, Most-Great, Hu, in majesty

جَلِيلٍ جَلَّ جَلْيُوتٍ جَمًّا تَمَهْرَجَتْ

Jalīlin jalla Jalyūtin jamman tamahrajat
Most-Noble, Exalted, Jalyut, in intense battles

تُقَادُ سِرَاجَ السُّرْجِ سِرًّا بَيَانَةً

Tuqādu sirāja-s-surji sirran bayānatan
The lamp of lamps is guided in a clear secret

تُقَادُ سِرَاجَ السُّرْجِ سِرًّا تَنَوَّرَتْ

Tuqādu sirāja-s-surji sirran tanawwarat
The lamp of lamps is guided in a glowing secret

بِتَعْدَادِ أَبْرُومٍ وَسِمْرَازِ أَبْرَمٍ

Bi-taʿdādi Abrūmin wa Simrāzi Abramin
By the numbers of Abrum and the Returner of Abram

وَبَهْرَةِ تَبْرِيزٍ وَأُمٍّ تَبَرَّكَتْ

Wa bahrati tabrīzin wa ummin tabarrakat
And the Bahrat of Tabriz and a blessed mother

بِنُورِ جَمَالٍ بَازِخٍ وَشَرَنْطَخٍ

Bi-nūri jamālin bāzikhin wa sharanṭakhin
By the light of beauty, illumined and vast

بِقَدُّوسٍ بَرْهُوتٍ بِهِ الظُّلْمَةُ انْجَلَتْ

Bi-Qaddūsin Barhūtin bihi-ẓ-ẓulmatu-n-jalat
By the Most-Holy and Barhut
through whom darkness is lifted

بِآلٍ أَهِيلٍ شَلْعٍ شَلْعُوبٍ شَالِعٍ

Bi-Ālin Ahīlin Shalʿin Shalʿūbin Shāliʿin
By the noble family, the Most-Merciful,
Most-Beneficent, and the Real

طَهِيٍّ طَهُوبٍ طَيْطَهُوبٍ تَطَيْطَهَتْ

Ṭahiyyin Ṭahūbin Ṭayṭahūbin Taṭayṭahat
O Most-Beautiful and Answerer, respond with beauty

اَنُوخٍ بَيْمَلُوخٍ وَابْرُوخٍ أُقْسِمَتْ

Anūkhin Baymalūkhin wa Abrūkhin uqsimat
O Singular, the One, elevate me to the Beloved

بِتَمْلِيخِ آيَاتٍ شَمُوخٍ تَشَلْمَخَتْ

Bi-tamlīkhi āyātin Shamūkhin tashalmakhat
By the movement of signs, lofty and elevated

اَبَازِيخِ بَيْذُوخٍ وَدَيْمُوخٍ بَعْدَهَا

Abāzīkhi baydhūkhin wa daymūkhin baʿdahā
By the Abazikh of Baydhukh and Daymukh thenceforth

خَمَارُوخٍ بَشْرُوخٍ بِشَرْخٍ تَشَمَّخَتْ

Khamārūkhin Bashrūkhin bi-Sharkhin tashammakhat
Khamarukh, Bashrukh and a lofty abyss

بِبَلْخٍ وَسِمْيَانٍ وَبَازُوخٍ بَعْدَهَا

Bi-Balkhin wa Simyānin wa Bāzūkhin baʿdahā
By Balkh, Simyan and Bazukh thenceforth

بِزَيْمُوخٍ اَشْمُوخٍ بِهِ الْكَوْنُ عُمِّرَتْ

Bi-Zaymūkhin Ashmūkhin bihi-l-kawnu ʿummirat
By the Highest Deputy, Singular,
through whom the universe prospered

بِشَلْمَخَتٍ اِقْبَلْ دُعَائِي وَكُنْ مَعِي

Bi-Shalmakhatin iqbal duʿāʾī wa kun maʿī
O my Lord, accept my supplication and be with me

وَكُنْ لِي مِنَ الْأَعْدَاءِ حَسْبِي فَقَدْ بَغَتْ

Wa kun lī mina-l-aʿdāʾi ḥasbī fa-qad baghat
And be for me, suffice me from enemies
who have transgressed

اَنُوخٍ بَيْمَلُوخٍ بَرُوخٍ وَبَرْخُوا

Anūkhin Baymalūkhin Barūkhin wa Barkhū
By Anukh, the Returner, All-Able, and Most-Capable

بِتَمْلَاخِ يَايَاهٍ شَمُوخٍ تَشَامَخَتْ

Bi-Tamlākhi Yāyāhin Shamūkhin Tashāmakhat
O All-Knower, our Dependence, Most-Lofty and Elevated

فَيَا شَمْلَخَا يَا شَمْلَخَا أَنْتَ شَمْلَخَا

Fa-yā Shamlakhā yā Shamlakhā Anta Shamlakhā
O Most-Merciful, You are the Most-Merciful

وَيَا عَيْطَلَا غَوْثِ الرِّيَاحِ تَخَلْخَلَتْ

Wa yā ʿAyṭalā Ghawthi-r-riyāḥi takhalkhalat
O Most-Strong, the Succor of winds made lofty and mixed

وَيَا تَمْلَخَيَاهٍ فَهَا أَنْتَ تَمْلَخَا

Wa yā Tamlakhayāhin fa-hā Anta Tamlakhā
O All-Knowing, You are the All-Knower

وَيَا شَمْخَثِيْثَا تِلْكَ ذَاتٍ تَنَوَّرَتْ

Wa yā Shamkhathīthā tilka Dhātin tanawwarat
O Great in Light, that is an Illumined Essence

بِيَاهٍ وَيَايُوهٍ نَمُوهٍ اَصَالِيًا

Bi-Yāhin wa Yāyūhin Namūhin Aṣāliyan
O our Dependence, Yuhin, Namuh and Asal

نَجَا عَالِيًا يَسِّرْ أُمُورِي بِصَلْصَلَتْ

Najā ʿāliyan yassir umūrī bi-Ṣalṣalat
Grant me Your Swift Aid, and facilitate my affairs
O Swift in Punishment

وَاحْرُسْنِي يَا ذَا الْجَلَالِ بِكُنْ وَكُنْ

Wa-ḥrusnī yā Dha-l-Jalāli bi-kun wa kun
Protect me, O Most-Exalted, through Be! And Be!

بِنَصٍّ حَكِيْمٍ قَاطِعِ السِّرِ اَسْبَلَتْ

Bi-naṣṣin ḥakīmin qāṭiʿi-s-sirri asbalat
By the words of wisdom that have
unfolded a deafening secret

بِكَ الْحَوْلُ وَالطَّوْلُ الشَّدِيدُ لِمَنْ أَتَى

Bika-l-ḥawlu wa-ṭ-ṭawlu-sh-shadīdu li-man atā
Through You are all means, intense sufficiency
for all those who come

لِبَابِكَ يَرْجُوا جَاهَكَ الظُّلْمَةُ انْجَلَتْ

Li-bābika yarjū jāhaka-ẓ-ẓulmatu-n-jalat
To Your Door, seeking Your Protection,
through which darkness is lifted

حُرُوفٍ لِبِهْرَامٍ عَلَتْ وَتَشَامَخَتْ

Ḥurūfin li-Bihrāmin ʿalat wa tashāmakhat
The letters of Bihram elevated and made lofty

بِأَسْمَا عَصَى مُوسَى بِهَا الظُّلْمَةُ انْجَلَتْ

Bi-asmā ʿaṣā Mūsā biha-ẓ-ẓulmatu-n-jalat
By the names of Moses' staff,
through which darkness is lifted

تَوَسَّلْتُ بِالْأَقْسَامِ رَبِّي بِحَقِّهَا

Tawassaltu bi-l-aqsāmi Rabbī bi-ḥaqqihā
I seek the intercession of these oaths,
my Lord, by their stations

بِفَضْلِ جَلَالِ اللهِ بِالْخَيْرِ قَدْ أَتَتْ

Bi-faḍli Jalāli-l-Lāhi bi-l-khayri qad atat
By the bounty of God's Majesty,
through which all goodness has come

بِحَقِّ لَلْطَهْطِيلٍ مَهْطَهْطِيلٍ بَعْدَهَا

Bi-ḥaqqi lalṭahṭīlin mahṭahṭīlin baʿdahā
By the status of Laltahtil and Mahtahtil thenceforth

بِحَقِّ قَهْطَهْطِيلٍ فَهْطَهْطِيلٍ اَرْبَعَتْ

Bi-ḥaqqi qahṭahṭīlin fahtahtīlin arbaʿat
By the status of Qahtahtil and Fahtahtil the fourth

بِحَقِّ نَهْطَهْطِيلٍ جَهْطَهْطِيلٍ سَادِسٌ

Bi-ḥaqqi nahṭahṭīlin jahṭahṭīlin sādisun
By the status of Nahtahtil and Jahtahtil the sixth

بِحَقِّ لَهْطَهْطِيلٍ لِـمُقْفَنْجَلٍ جُمِّعَتْ

Bi-ḥaqqi lahṭahṭīlin li-muqfanjalin jummiʿat
By the status of Lahtahtil and Muqfanjal, all gathered

مَلَكْتُ بِمِيمِ الْمُلْكِ سَيْفًا مُجَرَّدًا

Malaktu bi-mīmi-l-mulki sayfan mujarradan
I own, through the Mim of dominion, a bared sword

أَصُولُ بِهِ قَهْرًا عَلَى الْإِنْسِ وَالْجِنِّ إِنْ بَغَتْ

Aṣūlu bihi qahran ʿala-l-insi wa-l-jinni in baghat
With it I subject Mankind and Jinn if they transgress

وَقَوِّمْنِي الْقَيُّومُ بِالْقَافِ قَاهِرًا

Wa qawwimni-l-Qayyūmu bi-l-qāfi qāhiran
Establish me, O Everlasting, through Qaf, as a subduer

ظَهُورًا لِلْأَعْدَاءِ وَالرِّقَابِ تَقَطَّعَتْ

Ẓahūran li-l-aʿdāʾi wa-r-riqābi taqaṭṭaʿat
Confronting enemies, as their honor is humiliated

اَلْمُرُوَّةُ لِلّٰهِ لَا شَيْءَ غَيْرُهُ

Al-muruwwatu li-l-Lāhi lā shayʾa ghayruhu
Chivalry is God's alone, there is naught but Him

حُبِّبْتُ لِنُورِ الرُّوحِ وَالْإِسْمِ قَدْ عَلَتْ

Ḥubbibtu li-nūri-r-rūḥi wa-l-Ismi qad ʿalat
I'm made beloved to the light of the spirit
and the Name as it ascends

فَتِلْكَ حُرُوفُ النُّورِ فَاجْمَعْ خَوَاصَّهَا

Fa-tilka ḥurūfu-n-nūri fa-j-maʿ khawāṣṣihā
Those are the letters of light, so gather their traits

وَحَقِّقْ مَعَانِيْهَا بِهَا الْخَيْرُ تُمِّمَتْ

Wa ḥaqqiq maʿānīhā biha-l-khayru tummimat
And actualize their meanings,
through which goodness is complete

أَوَائِلُ سُوَرِ الذِّكْرِ تَقْرَا فَوَاتِحًا

Awāʾilu suwari-dh-dhikri taqrā fawātiḥan
Recite the beginnings of the chapters of the Qur'an

لِإِشْرَاقِ مَا فِيْهَا مِنَ النُّورِ أَشْرَقَتْ

Li-ishrāqi mā fīhā mina-n-nūri ashraqat
By the illumination of the lights that glow therein

بِأَلِفٍ وَلَامٍ ثُمَّ مِيمٍ عَلَى الْوَلَى

Bi-alifin wa lāmin thumma mīmin ʿala-l-walā
By Alif, Lam then Mim in sequence

أَنَالُ بِهَا مَا تَشْتَهِي النَّفْسُ أَوْ سَعَتْ

Anālu bihā mā tashtahi-n-nafsu aw saʿat
I obtain what the soul desires and sought after

بِأَلِفٍ وَلَامٍ وَالنِّسَاءُ عُقُودُهَا

Bi-alifin wa lāmin wa-n-nisāʾu ʿuqūduhā
By Alif, Lam, the 'Women' and its oaths

وَفِي سُورَةِ الْأَنْعَامِ وَالنُّورُ نُوِّرَتْ

Wa fī sūrati-l-anʿāmi wa-n-nūru nuwwirat
In the chapter of the 'Cattle' as the light illumines

بِأَلِفٍ وَلَامٍ ثُمَّ مِيمٍ وَصَادِهَا

Bi-alifin wa lāmin thumma mīmin wa ṣādihā
By Alif, Lam then Mim and its Sad

عَلَوْتُ بِهَا فَخْرًا وَذَاتِي تَنَوَّرَتْ

ʿAlawtu bihā fakhran wa dhātī tanawwarat
I elevated through it in pride and essence illumined

بِأَلِفٍ وَلَامٍ ثُمَّ رَاءٍ بِسِرِّهَا

Bi-alifin wa lāmin thumma rāʾin bi-sirrihā
By Alif, Lam then Raʾ and its secret

عَلَوْتُ بِنُورِ الْإِسْمِ مِنْ كُلِّ مَا خَبَتْ

ʿAlawtu bi-nūri-l-Ismi min kulli mā khabat
I elevated, through the light of the Name
from all that is hidden

بِأَلِفٍ وَلَامٍ ثُمَّ مِيْمٍ وَرَائِهَا

Bi-alifin wa lāmin thumma mīmin wa rāʾihā
By Alif, Lam then Mim and its Raʾ

إِلَى مَجْمَعِ الْأَرْوَاحِ وَالرُّوحُ قَدْ عَلَتْ

Ilā majmaʿi-l-arwāḥi wa-r-rūḥu qad ʿalat
To the gathering of spirits as the spirit ascends

بِكَافٍ وَهَايَا ثُمَّ عَيْنٍ وَصَادِهَا

Bi-kāfin wa hāyā thumma ʿaynin wa ṣādihā
By Kaf, Ha, Ya then ʿAyn and its Sad

كِفَايَتُنَا مِنْ كُلِّ عَيْنٍ بِنَا حَوَتْ

Kifāyatunā min kulli ʿaynin binā ḥawat
It is our sufficiency from every evil eye that surrounds us

بِطٰهٰ وَيَاسِينِ وَطَاسِينِ تَكُنْ لَنَا

Bi-ṭāhā wa yāsīni wa ṭasīni takun lanā
By Ta-Ha, Ya-Sin and Ta-Sin be for us

وَطَاسِينِ مِيمٍ بِالسَّعَادَةِ اَقْبَلَتْ

Wa ṭāsīni mīmin bi-s-saʿādati aqbalat
And Ta-Sin-Mim came forth with joy

بِسِرِّ حَوَامِيمِ الْكِتَابِ جَمِيعِهَا

Bi-sirri ḥawāmīmi-l-kitābi jamīʿihā
By the secret of all the book's Ha-Mim

عَلَيْكَ بِفَضْلِ النُّورِ يَا نُورُ أُقْسِمَتْ

ʿAlayka bi-faḍli-n-nūri yā nūru uqsimat
By the bounty of light, O Light, we ask You

بِحَامِيمِ عَيْنٍ ثُمَّ بِسِينٍ وَقَافِهَا

Bi-ḥāmīmi ʿaynin thumma bi-sīnin wa qāfihā
By Ha, Mim, ʿAyn then by Sin and its Qaf

حِمَايَتُنَا مِنْ كُلِّ سُوءٍ بِشَلْمَهَتْ

ḥimāyatunā min kulli sūʾin bi-Shalmahat
is our protection from every harm, O Opener

بِقَافٍ وَنُونٍ ثُمَّ حَامِيمٍ بَعْدَهَا

Bi-qāfin wa nūnin thumma ḥāmīmin baʿdahā
By Qaf, Nun then Ha-Mim thenceforth

وَفِي سُورَةِ الدُّخَانِ سِرًّا قَدْ أُحْكِمَتْ

Wa fī sūrati-d-dukhāni sirran qad uḥkimat
In the chapter of 'The Smoke' is a guarded secret

وَالذَّارِيَاتِ ذَرْوًا وَالنَّجْمِ إِذَا هَوَى

Wa-dh-dhāriyāti dharwan wa-n-najmi idhā hawā
By 'The Winds' that disperse and 'The Star' when it falls

وَبِاقْتَرَبَتْ لِيَ الأُمُورُ تَقَرَّبَتْ

Wa bi-qtarabat liya-l-umūru taqarrabat
And by it has drawn near [The Moon], my affairs are near

بِحَقِّ تَبَارَكَ ثُمَّ نُونٍ وَسَائِلٍ

Bi-ḥaqqi Tabāraka thumma nūnin wa sāʾilin
By 'The Dominion' then 'Nun' and 'The Ascensions'

وَفِي سُورَةِ التَّهْمِيزِ وَالشَّمْسِ كُوِّرَتْ

Wa fī sūrati-t-tahmīzi wa-sh-shamsi kuwwirat
By the status of the chapters
'The Backbiter' and 'The Dimming'

بِعَمَّ وَعَبَسَ وَالنَّازِعَاتِ وَطَارِقٍ

Bi-ʿamma wa ʿabasa wa-n-nāziʿāti wa ṭāriqin
By 'The News', 'He Frowned',
'The Stripping Angels' and 'The Knocker'

وَفِي السَّمَاءِ ذَاتِ الْبُرُوجِ وَزُلْزِلَتْ

Wa fi-s-samāʾi dhāti-l-burūji wa zulzilat
And 'The Constellations' and 'The Quakening'

وَفِي سُورَةِ الْقُرْآنِ حَرْفًا مُجَرَّدًا

Wa fī sūrati-l-qurʾāni ḥarfan mujarradan
In the chapter 'The Criterion' is a manifest letter

عَدَدَ مَا قَرَى الْقَارِئُ وَمَا قَدْ تَنَزَّلَتْ

ʿAdada mā qara-l-qāriʾu wa mā qad tanazzalat
In what every reciter reads and what has descended

سَأَلْتُكَ يَا مَوْلَايَ فِي فَضْلِكَ الَّذِي

Saʾaltuka yā Mawlāya fī faḍlika-l-ladhī
I ask You, O my Guardian, by Your Bounty

عَلَى كُلِّ مَا أَنْزَلْتَ كِتَابًا تَفَضَّلَتْ

ʿAlā kulli mā anzalta kitāban tafaḍḍalat
By every Holy Book that You have sent with Your Bounty

بِآهِيَا شَرَاهِيًا اَذُو نَائِ صَبْوَةٍ

Bi-āhiyā sharāhiyan a-dhū nāʾyi ṣabwatin
By Ahya Sharahya and Adonai of youth

بِعِزَّةِ آلٍ شَدَائِيَ قَدْ تَجَمَّعَتْ

Bi-ʿizzati ālin shadāʾiya qad tajammaʿat
By the exaltedness of noble families
my strength is gathered

بِسِرِّ بَدُّوحٍ أَجْهَزَطٍ بَطَدٍ زَهَجٍ

Bi-sirri Baddūḥin Ajhazaṭin Baṭadin Zahajin
By the secret of Badduh, Ajhazat, Batad and Zahaj

بِوَاحِ الْوَحَا وَالنَّصْرِ وَالْفَتْحِ قَدْ حَوَتْ

Bi-wāḥi-l-waḥā wa-n-naṣri wa-l-fatḥi qad ḥawat
By the Wah of Waha, victory and contained opening

بِفَرْدٍ وَجَبَّارٍ شَهِيدٍ وَثَابِتٍ

Bi-Fardin wa Jabbārin Shahīdin wa Thābitin
By the Singular, All-Powerful, the Witness and Firm

ظَهِيرٍ خَبِيرٍ بِزَكِيٍّ تَجَمَّعَتْ

Ẓahīrin Khabīrin bi-Zakiyyin tajammaʿat
The Most-Apparent, All-Aware and Most-Pure gathered

بِحَقِّ فَقَجٍ مَعَ مَخْمَتٍ يَا إِلَهَنَا

Bi-ḥaqqi Faqajin maʿa Makhmatin yā Ilāhanā
By the Great Name, O our Lord

بِأَسْمَائِكَ الْعُظْمَى أَجِرْنَا مِنَ الشَّتَتَ

Bi-Asmāʾika-l-ʿUẓmā ajirnā mina-sh-shatat
By Your Great Names protect us from dispersion

بِنُورِ فَجَشٍ مَعَ ثَطْخَزٍ يَا سَيِّدِي

Bi-nūri fajashin maʿa thaṭkhazin yā Sayyidī
By the Light of the Greatest Name my Master

وَبِالْآيَةِ الْكُرْسِيِّ آمِنِّي مِنَ الْفَجَتَ

Wa bi-l-āyati-l-kursiyyi āminnī mina-l-fajat
By the verse of 'The Divine Seat', save me from harm

بِنُورِ جَلَالٍ وَنُورِ جَمَالٍ يَا إِلَهِي وَسَيِّدِي

Bi-nūri jalālin wa nūri jamālin yā Ilāhi wa Sayyidī
By the Lights of Majesty and Beauty, my Lord and Master

وَبِالْآيَةِ الْكُبْرَى آمِنِّي مِنَ الْفَجَتْ

Wa bi-l-āyati-l-kubrā āminnī mina-l-fajat
By the Great Verse save me from harm

تَوَسَّلْتُ إِلَيْكَ مَوْلَانَا بِسِرِّهَا

Tawassaltu ilayka Mawlānā bi-sirrihā
I ask You, my Guardian, by their secrets

تَوَسُّلِ ذِي ذُلٍّ بِهِ النَّاسُ اهْتَدَتْ

Tawassuli dhī dhullin bihi-n-nāsu-htadat
The seeking of a humbled guide for the people

حُرُوفٍ بِمَعْنَاهَا لَهَا الْفَضْلُ شُرِّفَتْ

Ḥurūfin bi-maʿnāhā laha-l-faḍlu shurrifat
Letters in whose meanings are ennobled bounties

مَدَدَ الدَّهْرِ وَالْأَيَّامِ يَا رَبِّ انْجَلَتْ

Madada-d-dahri wa-l-ayyāmi yā Rabbi-njalat
Throughout time and days, O my Lord, lift the burdens

فَسَخِّرْ لِي فِيهَا خَدِيمًا يُطِيعُنِي

Fa-sakhkhir lī fīhā khadīman yuṭīʿunī
Make for me, through it, a servant that obeys me

بِفَضْلِ حُرُوفِ أُمِّ الْقُرْآنِ وَمَا تَلَتْ

Bi-faḍli ḥurūfi ummi-l-qurʾāni wa mā talat
By the bounty of the letters
of the Mother of the Quran and what it recites

بِفَضْلِ كِتَابِ اللهِ بِالْقُدْرَةِ الَّتِي

Bi-faḍli kitābi-l-Lāhi bi-l-qudrati-l-latī
By the bounty of God's Book and its power

بِهَا الْأَرْضُ مُدَّتْ وَالْجِبَالُ تَشَمَّخَتْ

Biha-l-arḍu muddat wa-l-jibālu tashammakhat
With which the earth extended and mountains elevated

بِحَقِّكَ بِالْأَمْلَاكِ وَالرُّسْلِ كُلِّهِمْ

Bi-ḥaqqika bi-l-amlāki wa-r-rusli kullihim
By Your Truth, Angels and all Messengers

بِحُرْمَةِ يَوْمِ الْحَشْرِ وَالْخَلْقِ جُمِّعَتْ

Bi-ḥurmati yawmi-l-ḥashri wa-l-khalqi jummiʿat
By the sanctity of the Day of Gathering
when all people are brought together

بِيَاهٍ نَمُوهٍ مَعَ أَواهٍ جَمِيعُهَا

Bi-Yāhin Namūhin maʿa Awāhin jamīʿuhā
O our Dependence, Most-Praiseworthy and Awah

بِهَكْشَخٍ هَكْشَاخٍ كَنُونٍ تَكَوَّنَتْ

Bi-Hakshakhin Hakshākhin ka-nūnin takawwanat
By 'Be!' and 'it is' as a Nun is formed

وَأَسْأَلُكَ يَا مَوْلَايَ فِي اِسْمِكَ الَّذِي

Wa asʾaluka yā Mawlāya fī Ismika-l-ladhī
I ask You, my Master, by Your Name

بِهِ إِذَا دُعِيَ جَمِيعُ الْأُمُورِ تَيَسَّرَتْ

Bihi idhā duʿiya jamīʿu-l-umūri tayassarat
Through which all affairs are facilitated

وَتَرْحَمُ ضَعْفِي يَا إِلَٰهِي وَذِلَّتِي

Wa tarḥamu ḍaʿfī yā Ilāhī wa dhillatī
That You show mercy for my weakness and abasement

بِمَا قَدْ دَعَاكَ الْأَنْبِيَاءُ تَوَسَّلَتْ

Bi-mā qad daʿāka-l-anbiyāʾu tawassalat
By all that prophets have called upon You

أَيَا خَالِقِي وَيَا سَيِّدِي اِقْضِ حَاجَتِي

A-yā Khāliqī wa yā Sayyidī iqḍi ḥājatī
My Creator and Master, fulfill my needs

إِلَيْكَ أُمُورِى يَا إِلَٰهِي تَسَلَّمَتْ

Ilayka umūrī yā Ilāhī tasallamat
To You, my God, are my affairs delivered

تَوَسَّلْتُ يَا رَبِّي إِلَيْكَ بِأَحْمَدٍ

Tawassaltu yā Rabbī ilayka bi-Aḥmadin
I ask You, O my Lord, by Ahmad ﷺ

وَاَسْمَائِكَ الْحُسْنَى الَّتِي هِيَ جُمِّعَتْ

Wa Asmāʾika-l-Ḥusnā al-latī hiya jummiʿat
And Your Beautiful Names, all gathered

لَا إِلَٰهَ إِلَّا أَنْتَ يَا حَيُّ يَا قَيُّومُ

Lā ilāha illā Anta yā Ḥayyu yā Qayyūmu
There is no god but You, Eternally-Living and Everlasting

وَأَنْتَ حَسْبِي رَبِّ جَلَّ اللهُ جَلْجَلَتْ

Wa Anta ḥasbī Rabbi jalla Allāhu Jaljalat
You are my Sufficiency, my Lord, may God be Exalted

فَجُدْ وَاعْفُ وَامْنَحْ يَا إِلَهِي بِتَوْبَةٍ

Fa-jud wa-ʿfu wa-mnaḥ yā Ilāhī bi-tawbatin
Show generosity, forgiveness
and grant, O my Lord, a repentance

عَلَى عَبْدِكَ الْمِسْكِينِ مِنْ نَظْرَةٍ نَمَتْ

ʿAlā ʿabdika-l-miskīni min naẓratin namat
For Your weak servant, with Your Increasing Gaze

وَلِلْخَيْرِ وَفِّقْنِي وَالصِّدْقِ وَالتُّقَى

Wa li-l-khayri waffiqnī wa-ṣ-ṣidqi wa-t-tuqā
Facilitate me to goodness, truthfulness and piety

وَاَسْكِنِّيَ الْفِرْدَوْسَ مَعَ فِرْقَةٍ عَلَتْ

Wa askinniya-l-firdawsa maʿa firqatin ʿalat
Grant me residence in a paradise with a lofty group

وَكُنْ لِي رَؤُوفًا فِي حَيَاتِي وَبَعْدَ مَا

Wa kun lī Raʾūfan fī ḥayātī wa baʿda mā
Be kind with me, in this life and thereafter

أَمُوتُ وَارْفَعْ ظُلْمَةَ الْقَبْرِ وَالْخَلَتْ

Amūtu wa-rfaʿ ẓulmatu-l-qabri wa-l-khalat
When I die, and lift the darkness
of my grave and loneliness

وَفِي الْحَشْرِ يَا إِلَهِي بَيِّضْ صَحِيْفَتِي

Wa fi-l-ḥashri yā Ilāhī bayyiḍ ṣaḥīfatī
In the Resurrection, my God, clean my parchment

وَثَقِّلْ مَوَازِينِي بِفَضْلِكَ وَانْجَلَتْ

Wa thaqqil mawāzīnī bi-faḍlika wa-njalat
Make my scale heavy with Your Bounty,
and lift my burdens

وَجَوِّزْنِي عَلَى حَدِّ الصِّرَاطِ مُهَرْوِلًا

Wa jawwiznī ʿalā ḥaddi-ṣ-ṣirāti muharwilan
Let me pass over the bridge running

فَيَحْفَظُنِي مِنْ حَرِّ نَارٍ وَمَا حَوَتْ

Fa-yaḥfaẓunī min ḥarri nārin wa mā ḥawat
And protect me from the fire's heat and what it contains

تُسَامِحْنِي مِنْ كُلِّ ذَنْبٍ جَنَيْتُهُ

Tusāmiḥnī min kulli dhanbin janaytuhu
Forgive me for every sin I have committed

وَتَعْفُ عَنْ خَطِيْئَاتِي الْعِظَامِ وَإِنْ عَلَتْ

Wa taʿfu ʿan khaṭīʾāti-l-ʿiẓāmi wa in ʿalat
Look over my great mistakes, despite their gravity

فَيَا حَامِلَ الْإِسْمِ الَّذِي جَلَّ قَدْرُهُ

Fa-yā ḥāmila-l-Ismi-l-ladhī jalla qadruhu
So You, who carries the Lofty Name

تَوَفَّى بِهِ كُلَّ الْأُمُورِ تَسَلَّمَتْ

Tawaffā bihi kulla-l-umūri tasallamat
Fulfill your needs, through it all affairs are safe

وَلَا تَخْشَ مِنْ سَيْفٍ وَلَا طَعْنِ خَنْجَرٍ

Wa lā takhsha min sayfin wa lā ṭaʿni khanjarin
Do not fear a sword nor the stab of a knife

وَلَا تَخْشَ مِنْ رُمْحٍ وَلَا شَرِّ أَسْهَمَتْ

Wa lā takhsha min rumḥin wa lā sharri as-hamat
And fear neither a spear nor evil's arrow

فَلَا حَيَّةٌ تَخْشَى وَلَا عَقْرَبٌ تَرَى

Fa-lā ḥayyatun takhshā wa lā ʿaqrabun tarā
And fear neither a snake nor a scorpion you see

وَلَا أَسَدٌ يَأْتِي إِلَيْكَ بِهَمْهَمَتْ

Wa lā asadun yaʾtī ilayka bi-hamhamat
Nor a roaring lion that leaps at you

فَقَاتِلْ وَلَا تَخْشَ وَحَارِبْ وَلَا تَخَفْ

Fa-qātil wa lā takhsha wa ḥārib wa lā takhaf
So fight, do not be frightened and battle without fear

وَدُسْ كُلَّ أَرْضٍ بِالْوُحُوشِ تَعَمَّرَتْ

Wa dus kulla arḍin bi-l-wuḥūshi taʿammarat
And step upon every land filled with monsters

وَأَقْبِلْ وَلَا تَهْرَبْ وَخَاصِمْ مَنْ تَشَا

Wa aqbil wa lā tahrab wa khāṣim man tashā
Come forth, do not run away
and show enmity to whomever you will

وَلَا تَخْشَ بَأْسًا لِلْمُلُوكِ وَلَوْ حَوَتْ

Wa lā takhsha baʾsan li-l-mulūki wa law ḥawat
Do not fear the might of kings even if they overwhelm you

ثَلَاثَ عُصِيٍّ صُفِّفَتْ بَعْدَ خَاتَمٍ

Thalātha ʿusiyyin ṣuffifat baʿda khātamin
Three staves aligned following a ring

عَلَى رَأْسِهَا مِثْلُ السِّنَانِ تَشَرْبَكَتْ

ʿAlā raʾsihā mithlu-s-sināni tasharbakat
On their heads are colliding teeth

وَمِيمٌ طَمِيسٌ أَبْتَرٌ ثُمَّ سُلَّمٌ

Wa mīmun ṭamīsun abtarun thumma sullamun
A concealed and cut Mim with a ladder

وَفِي وَسْطِهَا بِالْحَرْبَتَيْنِ تَقَوَّمَتْ

Wa fī wasṭihā bi-l-ḥarbatayni taqawwamat
In the middle are two standing spears

وَأَرْبَعَةٌ تَحْكِي الْأَنَامِلَ بَعْدَهَا

Wa arbaʿatun taḥki-l-anāmila baʿdahā
And four whose tales fingers foretell

تُشِيرُ إِلَى الْخَيْرَاتِ وَالرِّزْقِ جُمِّعَتْ

Tushīru ila-l-khayrāti wa-r-rizqi jummiʿat
They point to goodness and gathered wealth

وَهَاءٌ شَفِيْقٌ ثُمَّ وَاوٌ مُقَوَّسٌ

Wa hāʾun shafīqun thumma wāwun muqawwasun
Then a kind Ha and an arched Waw

كَأَنْبُوبِ حَجَّامٍ مِنَ السِّرِ الْتَوَتْ

Ka-anbūbi ḥajjāmin mina-s-sirri-l-tawat
Like a copper's tube filled with secrets

وَآخِرُهَا مِثْلُ الْأَوَائِلُ خَاتَمٌ

Wa ākhiruhā mithlu-l-awāʾilu khātamun
At their end, like the beginning, is a ring

خُمَاسِيٌّ أَرْكَانٌ بِهِ السِّرُّ قَدْ حَوَتْ

Khumāsiyyun arkānun bihi-s-sirru qad ḥawat
With five sides, its pillars surrounded with the secret

وَلَا إِلَهَ إِلَّا اللهُ جَلَّ جَلَالُهُ

Wa lā ilāha illa-l-Lāhu jalla Jalāluhu
There is no god but God, may He be Exalted

مُحَمَّدٌ رَسُوْلُ اللهِ حَقًّا وَحُقِّقَتْ

Muḥammadu-r-rasūlu-l-Lāhi ḥaqqan wa ḥuqqiqat
Muhammad ﷺ is the messenger of God,
truthfully and realized

Milton Keynes UK
Ingram Content Group UK Ltd.
UKHW051014191124
2941UKWH00023B/92

9 781938 058813